How to Scratch a Wombat

WHERE TO FIND IT . . . WHAT TO FEED IT . . .

WHY IT SLEEPS ALL DAY

by Jackie French

Illustrated by Bruce Whatley

Clarion Books

New York

Clarion Books

an imprint of Houghton Mifflin Harcourt Publishing Company

215 Park Avenue South, New York, NY 10003

Text copyright © 2005, 2009 by Jackie French

Illustrations copyright © 2005, 2009 by Farmhouse Illustration Company Pty Ltd.

Adapted from *The Secret World of Wombats*, first published in
Sydney, Australia, by HarperCollins Publishers Australia Pty Ltd., in 2005.
This edition is published by arrangement with HarperCollins Publishers Australia Pty Ltd.
First American edition, 2009.

The illustrations were executed in pencil, pen and ink, and acrylic paint.
The text was set in 13-point Berkeley Book.

www.clarionbooks.com

Printed in the U.S.A.

Library of Congress Cataloging-in-Publication Data

French, Jackie.
How to scratch a wombat : where to find it . . . what to feed it . . . why it sleeps all day /
by Jackie French ; illustrated by Bruce Whatley. —1st American ed.
p. cm.
ISBN 978-0-618-86864-3
1. Wombats—Juvenile literature. I. Whatley, Bruce, ill. II. Title.

QL737.M39F74 2009
599.2'4—dc22
2008002581

WOZ 10 9 8 7 6 5 4 3 2 1

To Smudge, Fudge, Pudge, Chocolate,
Gabby, Bad Bart, Peanut, Mothball,
Golden Dragon, Two-and-a-Half,
Pretty Face, Flat White, Big Paws,
Grunter, Totally Confused, Whiskers,
Roadbat, and all the others—even Moriarty.
Thank you for so many years and a
glimpse into another universe.
—J.F.

Contents

Words to Know

bracken: a weedy fern

bum: bottom, buttocks

bush: a wilderness area

go bush: go, or return, to the wilderness

paddock: an enclosed field

pong: a strong smell, stink

rubbish: trash, garbage

scat: animal droppings, dung

sedge: grasslike plants with solid stems and leaves in three vertical rows

stroppy: bad tempered, ornery

torch: a flashlight

tucker: food

tussock: a clump or tuft of grass

①

Writing with Wombats

Down under my feet is a secret world. There are underground tunnels and hidden rooms and sleeping animals waiting for the night. It's the world of wombats.

If you're like most people, you've seen wombats only in books or in zoos. You haven't seen the secret side of wombats—wombat grins and wombat games. You don't know just how fascinating wombats are, or such things as:

- Why wombats bite each other's bums.
- How wombats "talk" to each other with their droppings.
- How singing is a wonderful way to get really close to a wombat.

I met my first wombat more than thirty years ago, when I was living in the Araluen Valley on the edge of the bush in New South Wales, Australia. I named the wombat Smudge, and we became friends. In fact, in many ways I think Smudge was the closest friend I've ever had. *And* he got me my first book published.

SMUDGE AND THE TYPEWRITER

The shed where I lived in those days was in the middle of Smudge's territory. Every evening he'd come inside and look around, and if I didn't leave the door open for him, he'd knock it down. Wombats are built like small furry tanks, and Smudge was a large wombat. Also, the door wasn't very strong. I had put it up myself, and I'm not much of a carpenter.

I hadn't meant to live in a shed. I'd planned to farm with my husband and live in a new house we'd build overlooking the creek. But the concrete foundation that the builder laid crumbled away when you stood on it. And by the time we got our money back, I was pregnant, and the marriage was nearly over. Then there was a drought, and our peach trees died.

I was broke. I needed $106.44 to register my car. And by now I had a baby to look after. Then I thought: *Maybe I can write a book.* I'd been writing stories all my life, just scribbling them on scraps of paper, but I'd never had the courage to send one to a publisher. Now I was desperate. But I couldn't send a scribbled-on bit of paper to a publisher, and there was no way I could afford to buy a typewriter.

In those days, I never went to the dump to leave rubbish. Jars and cans were used again, paper was turned into mulch, and all the food scraps went to the chickens. But I did stop off at the dump whenever I went to town, to see

if someone had left something useful—an old chair that I could repair or an old metal tank that I could patch with cement and use for storing water for the garden or for keeping firewood dry. And one morning there was a typewriter sitting in the middle of the pile. I clambered over a dead sheep and some smelly dog-food cans to retrieve it, hauled it back home, and tried it. It still worked!

I didn't have a desk. But I did have an old door. So I propped it up on stacks of bricks and put the typewriter on top. Then I sat down cross-legged on the floor and began to write my stories. Most of them were pretty bad— it had been years since I'd really worked at what I wrote. Still, I was extraordinarily happy to be writing again.

But Smudge hated that typewriter. Maybe he hated the noise—the *tappa, tappa, bing!* of an old-fashioned manual typewriter. Every night after I'd gone to bed, I'd hear him making his way around the shed. And every morning there'd be a large wombat dropping on the keys, just to make it clear that this was *his* territory, typewriter and all.

Every morning I'd clean off the wombat dropping and start work again. But after three months of wombat droppings, my "new" typewriter didn't work very well. In fact, the *E* key didn't work at all—it was soft and squishy when I pressed it. But all the other letters worked, so I kept writing.

Then one night, while I was sitting on a rock in the dry creek bed, watching Smudge nose about for shreds of grass, I remembered the rain stones I'd seen when I was working at a museum in Queensland. Rain stones are ancient sacred stones that have been kept by the elders of some aboriginal Australian nations for many, many generations. They are used to summon rain in times of drought. These particular stones were stored in a tobacco tin, with the label "On no account ever open to the air."

All at once I knew the story I wanted to write. It was about a girl who believes that the drought in her area will break if she can find an elder who will use his rain stones. But the only Aboriginal guy around is the local building inspector, who grew up in the city of Sydney, not in the bush.

I ran back to the shed and wrote *Rain Stones*. I knew this story had to be good—the best I was capable of writing. The land and the garden could feed me and my son. But if I didn't sell my book, there would be no car to take him to preschool, to the doctor if he needed it, to town where I might get part-time work as a cook.

Smudge followed me to the shed. He dozed on the

doorstep, twitching his nose in annoyance whenever the typewriter went *bing!* I finished the story that night; then I filled in all the missing E's by hand. It looked a bit messy . . . okay, very messy. The paper was old and yellow at the edges and had a few wombat-dropping smudges, and (I learned later) my spelling was terrible. I'm a very fast reader, but I've never been able to spell because I'm dyslexic—I have a learning disorder that affects how I see words. Still, it was the first story I'd written that hinted at the world I could picture in my mind's eye.

I had no idea how to get a book published, but I thought there were probably publishers in Sydney. I drove to the post office in town and looked up "publishers" in the Sydney telephone directory. The first one listed was Angus and Robertson. So I sent my story to them.

Years later, I heard what happened next. The editor who pulled my story out of the envelope yelled, "Hey, look at this, everyone! Look what someone has sent in!"

She said it was the worst-spelled, messiest manuscript anyone had ever submitted. And because it was so messy and the spelling so bad, she thought it would be unintentionally hilarious. So she sat down to read a bit out loud, so everyone could laugh at it. She read one paragraph. She read another. Then she read the whole story.

Three weeks later they sent me a check. They wanted to publish it. And they wanted more! Suddenly, I was a writer. I've been a full-time writer ever since—and I owe it all to Smudge.

MOTHBALL AND *DIARY OF A WOMBAT*

Nearly a quarter of a century has passed since *Rain Stones* was published . . . years filled with more books— and many more wombats.

I still live in the shed, but I share it with my second husband, Bryan, and it's different these days and much bigger. (Most people assume it's an old stone house that we've renovated and added to.) I've studied wombats, tracking them through the bush, watching and keeping notes, slowly becoming a "wombat expert," adding to the knowledge of these fascinating creatures. Over the years I've worked out ways that farmers and gardeners can grow vegetables, fruits, and flowers and coexist with Australian wildlife like wallabies and wombats without fencing them out or killing them.

I've also looked after orphaned baby wombats— cuddly, furry creatures that wreck your kitchen and take over your life. Gabby, Fuzzface, Pudge, Fudge, Rikki the

Wrestler, Chocolate—each one lived with us for months till it finally decided to take off into the bush, to live its life as a wild wombat.

And then there was Mothball.

Mothball was found in Canberra, badly mauled by dogs, bleeding, terrified, barely alive. Her rescuers raced her to a vet, who worked on her for hours, sewing up the gashes. Mothball was a determined little thing. Despite her injuries, she recovered. But she was badly scarred, and her fur came back in patches, as though it had been moth-eaten. So they called her Mothball.

"We'll miss her terribly. But at least we know she'll be going somewhere good," said her caretakers. Then they added, "By the way . . . she's very fond of carrots."

They gave me her blanket, with its rich, familiar wombat smell, and a couple of carrots to keep her happy. We put her in an animal carry cage on the back seat of my car, and I drove off to the sound of crunching. I'd just reached the outskirts of Canberra when the crunching stopped. Mothball had finished her carrots.

Hunh, hunh, hunh, hunh, hunh, she said from the back seat.

I ignored her.

Hunh, hunh, hunh, hunh, hunh! she said more loudly.

I waited for her to go to sleep.

Hunh, hunh, hunh, hunh, hunh!! She was angry now.

"Look," I said. "I don't have any more carrots! You'll have to wait until we get home."

Hunh, hunh, hunh, hunh, hunh!!! The cage rocked back and forth; then it tumbled onto the floor.

I screeched to a stop on the edge of the highway and peered into the back seat. Mothball appeared to be all right. "You have to be patient," I told her.

She gave an indignant screech in reply. Wombats are never patient.

I began to drive again. Ten miles . . . fifteen. . . .

Grg, grg, grg.

I glanced behind. Mothball was chewing on the plastic bars of the cage.

I did a quick calculation. If it takes one wombat ten minutes to chew through one bar of her cage, how long will it take her to chew through six bars . . . and climb *out* of the cage? Sixty minutes. But it would take me eighty minutes to get home. That left twenty minutes for a furious wombat to chew the car seats, the steering wheel, and me!

I stopped in Bungendore and bought more carrots—lots of carrots. I shoved them all into the cage.

Crunch. Crunch. Crunch. It was a happy sound, the sound of a wombat who is training her human to provide all the carrots she wants.

Mothball got fat on the soft green grass that grew around the house—and on the carrots she kept demanding. In time, she was almost totally circular, with tiny legs and a wombat grin. Her fur grew back a deep, rich brown.

Then she began to dig.

Mothball's first burrow was in the dust under the truck

in the shed. That hole collapsed when it was only seven or eight inches deep. But she kept on trying, night after night. All that grass-and-carrot energy had to be used up somehow.

Her second burrow was behind my study, in the herb garden. Mothball was a good digger. I went to bed one night with an herb garden and woke up the next morning with a big pile of dirt.

It took Mothball three nights to finish her hole. Then I put the sprinkler on the garden. Two minutes later, Mothball emerged, damp and disgusted. Her new burrow leaked!

This time Mothball decided to renovate an old wombat hole rather than dig another new one. Every morning Bryan carted away a wheelbarrow load of dirt and rocks that Mothball had cleared from the hole. Finally, she was ready to furnish her home. As I sat at my desk one day, I watched her pad back and forth between the garden and her hole, each time carrying a fresh branch of lavender to make her bed. It was the sweetest-smelling burrow around!

That winter we decided to build a new bedroom addition over the old herb garden, where Mothball had dug her second burrow. She hadn't even sniffed it since she'd moved out in disgust. Surely she wouldn't mind if we built there.

But as the carpenter put down the last of the flooring, a round brown wombat bum disappeared into the burrow below.

"She can't be moving back in!" said Bryan.

But she was. Somehow Mothball guessed that with the addition of a wide, thick roof, the burrow would no longer fill up with water. The trouble was, the burrow's entrance was exactly where the stairs were supposed to go. So either we had to move the house or move the wombat.

We moved the house. I already knew that there was no way on earth we could move Mothball.

She now had the fanciest wombat burrow in all of Australia. It had a concrete path to its door, a nice front patio, and a giant back veranda. She also had us trained to feed her carrots on demand. What a life!

I was on the phone with a friend one day, and every now and then I'd try to explain the noises she was overhearing and the sights I was seeing. "That's just Mothball bashing up the garbage bin so I'll bring her carrots out to her. . . . She's finished the carrots and she's eating grass. Now she's scratching. . . . Now she's bashing at the back

door to get more carrots. Oops! She's attacking the doormat. Oh, dear. She just chewed up a pair of jeans. . . ."

Suddenly, the idea for a story called *Diary of a Wombat* was born. I scribbled it down—there weren't many words—and sent it to my publisher. They loved it and hired Bruce Whatley to illustrate it.

I sent Bruce a pile of photos for reference, and some months later, his first rough sketches arrived at our post office box in town. I opened the parcel when I reached the car—and had to lean against the door, I was laughing so hard. The pictures were so funny and so perfect! He had captured Mothball exactly, but it was much more than that. He had simplified the wombat's outlines, played around with shadings . . . and suddenly there was magic.

Mothball's story won many awards in Australia. It's been translated into other languages for children around the world to enjoy. And it was on several best-book lists in the United States. But most people have no idea what a wombat is. Many think it's a type of small bear. So I wrote this book, a nonfiction companion to *Diary of a Wombat*.

Sometimes I think knowing wombats is as close as I'll ever come to meeting an alien. They are so different from us that it has taken me decades to understand the way they think and live. I hope the information in this book helps *you* understand the strange and wonderful world of wombats—and to love them as much as I do.

ARE YOU A WOMBAT?

`Are you covered in fur?`
No? Then you are definitely *not* a wombat—unless you are a bald wombat.

`Do you have a large egg-shaped brown nose?`
Yes? Then you might be a wombat —or a kid who has stuck his nose in a peanut butter jar.

`Do you come out mostly at night?`
Yes? Then you might be a wombat—or a vampire.

`Do you eat grass?`
Vampires hardly ever eat grass.

`Do you have tiny eyes, little ears, and an even smaller tail?`

`If you're a girl, do you have a pouch?`

`Do you have long claws and longer whiskers?`

`Do you live in a hole in the ground?`
If you've answered yes to all these questions, then you're a wombat. Or else you're a really weird kid!

② The History of Wombats

A hundred thousand years ago, a giant furry creature roamed the forests of Australia—places where there are only red sand hills now. The creature was as big as a hippopotamus, nearly ten feet long and about six and a half feet tall, with flat feet and a broad nose or maybe a short trunk. It was a *Diprotodon optatum,* and I'm glad we don't have one living under our house. (If a small wombat, like Mothball, can bite and claw her way through plastic bars, imagine what a *Diprotodon* would do if it wanted carrots!)

Diprotodon optatum was a close relative of modern wombats. There were many wombat-like animals back in ancient Australia. There were also giant kangaroos, massive echidnas, and marsupial lions. Some of these very large beasts—or megafauna—were still alive when humans came to Australia between 50,000 and 60,000 years ago. Some of those creatures were hunted and eaten. Others died as the climate became drier and there wasn't enough grass to feed on. Only *Diprotodon's* small relatives

Diprotodon optatum

survived: those with hairy noses, the *Lasiorhunis* wombats, and those with bare noses, *Vombatus ursinus*.

HUMANS AND WOMBATS

Aboriginal people hunted wombats and sometimes ate them, but probably only when other game was scarce. Wombats taste disgusting—they are mostly bone and gristle—and their fur feels like a shaggy doormat. Why bother with wombats if you can hunt kangaroo for meat and wear silky, soft koala or possum fur?

White settlers arrived in Australia in the late 1700s, but apparently it was years before they noticed wombats.

This isn't so very strange, as wombats are nocturnal animals. They live in their burrows during the day and come out mostly at night. It's hard to see a brown wombat on a black night unless you have a light of some kind. The early settlers were short of candles and oil for lamps, and they were nervous about the strange bush sounds around them. They just didn't go out much at night.

How did the wombat get its name? James Wilson, a former convict employed by John Hunter, governor of New South Wales from 1794 to 1800, came across one of the creatures on an expedition to the Blue Mountains. According to him, the local aboriginal people called it a *whom-batt*—and that's what it's been called ever since.

DANGEROUS TIMES FOR WOMBATS

Life changed for wombats when white settlers arrived. The settlers' cattle and sheep ate the wombats' grass, and the cattle's heavy feet flattened the wombats' burrows. The settlers brought rabbits, too, which ate more grass than the cattle and could feed in places that cattle and sheep couldn't reach.

Settlers trapped, poisoned, and shot wombats. Farmers still do so in many areas today, even where these actions are illegal. No fence stops a determined wombat, and farmers don't like holes in their fences, as their livestock can get through. Some farmers also resent any animal that eats grass, which they consider as belonging to their sheep and cattle.

Hairy-nosed wombat

Common wombat

Today, the southern hairy-nosed wombat (*Lasiorhinus latifrons*) lives only in a few spots around the Nullarbor Plain, and the northern hairy-nosed wombat (*Lasiorhinus krefftii*) is nearly extinct, surviving only in one colony in mid-north Queensland. The bare-nosed, or common, wombat (*Vombatus ursinus*), has done a bit better. You'll still find them in the wet forest areas of southeast New South Wales and Victoria and throughout Tasmania.

But overall, the wombat population is going down, mainly because of shooting, trapping, dog attacks, car incidents, fires (mostly lit by humans) that destroy large areas of bush and national parks, and competition from sheep and cattle. In many areas now, there aren't enough wombats to keep breeding.

Wombats can live for more than twenty years in zoos, but in the wild their life expectancy is much shorter. They live for about fourteen years around our valley, but in other regions they may live for only about five years, especially if it's dry and there isn't much grass.

This book is about common wombats. They're the ones you'll see most often in the bush or at the zoo. And they're the wombats I live with and have studied.

Northern Territory
Western Australia
Northern Hairy Nose
Southern Hairy Nose
Queensland
New South Wales
South Australia
Victoria
Common Wombat
Tasmania

WHO'S THE GREATEST – YOU OR A WOMBAT?

Can you scratch your ear with your (back) feet?
A wombat can.

Can you dig with your front feet (hands) while pushing dirt out with your back feet?
A wombat can.

Can you chew up tussock and digest it?
Do not try this!

Can you bite and claw your way through a door to get to the carrots?
Do not try this, either.

Can you leave a hundred droppings a night to mark your territory?
Definitely do not try this. Or if you do, don't say I told you to.

③

What Is a Wombat?

Wombats live in burrows and sleep—or at least are pretty dozy—during the day. If you see a wombat early in the evening, it'll probably be intent on eating. A wombat's closest relative is a koala, but wombats are much more intelligent than koalas. Their cerebral hemispheres (brains) are proportionately bigger than those of other marsupials. They are also determined and single-minded. Never get between a wombat and its burrow if the wombat wants to go there. You'll be knocked over!

Wombats think dirt is the most wonderful stuff in the world. They dust-bathe, wriggling on their backs or tummies in dry dirt or sand. This cleans their fur and helps get rid of ticks and mites. Old wombats especially love dust-bathing. They lie on their backs in warm dust, a bit like a person having a nice warm spa bath. Wombats also love freshly dug dirt. Gardening with a wombat is impossible. Every time you plant something, the wombat digs it up.

A WOMBAT'S BODY

Wombats are built for burrowing. They are digging ma-
chines. They have tiny eyes, small ears, short necks, and
strong, stocky bodies, with powerful shoulders and legs.
In fact, they look like hairy brown rocks with legs. But they
can squeeze through tiny gaps and flop down until they
are almost flat—their doormat position. Do not step on a
wombat! You'll regret it—and so will the wombat.

On average, adult wombats are a little over three feet
long, but like human height, this varies a lot. Some wombats are relatively small even when they are grown up;
others can grow to about four feet. Chocolate, the biggest
wombat I've ever known, was taller than my knees, with
shoulders like a sumo wrestler. Pretty Face, one of the
smallest, is only the size of a corgi, though she's a different shape. She also has the prettiest pointed nose and long
fluffy whiskers—she's a gorgeous wombat.

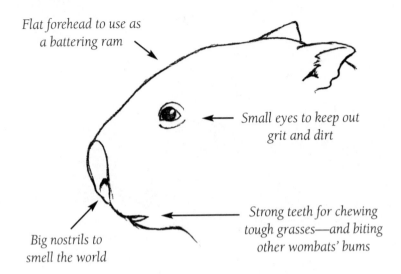

Flat forehead to use as a battering ram

Small eyes to keep out grit and dirt

Big nostrils to smell the world

Strong teeth for chewing tough grasses—and biting other wombats' bums

A WOMBAT'S FACE

Wombats have very strong, flattish skulls, which is a good thing, as they use their heads like battering rams. They charge headfirst through fences, screen doors, and kitchen cupboards, and they use their heads to knock down anyone who stands in their way.

Wombats have tiny eyes that they mostly keep closed, so grit can't get in them. The only vulnerable bit of a wombat's head is its ears. When wombats fight, they often try to bite each other's ears. But mostly they try to bite each other's bums. It's a lot easier to grab a wombat's bum than a wombat's head!

Wombats have broad, dry, leathery noses—pink when they are young and then dark brown as they get older. They have very big nostrils. If you look at a wombat skull, you'll see that the nostril openings are enormous. That's because smelling is the main way a wombat "sees" the world.

Wombats have dark narrow lips—and sometimes appear to grin.

A WOMBAT'S TEETH

Wombats have two giant lower teeth and two big upper teeth, set well apart from their other teeth. Their teeth keep growing all their lives and are ground down by the tough tussocks and other things they eat.

One of the ways wombats say hi is to give a nip. This doesn't hurt other wombats, because they have very tough skin. So they don't understand why people shriek in agony when their long teeth bite into human flesh.

BAD BART THE BITER

Bad Bart bit. He didn't mean to hurt. He was just saying hello. If you bent over in the garden, Bad Bart would bite your bum. If you sat in a garden chair, Bad Bart would bite your ankle. We had to warn visitors never to bend over in the garden and, if a wombat came nosing around the garden table, to lift their legs up high!

RIKKI THE WRESTLER

I have a scar on my left wrist from a wombat I called Rikki the Wrestler. Rikki loved wrestling—most young wombats do, especially males. Rikki used to grab my skirt and pull it until it tore. Or he would gallop up behind me and rip my jeans. One day I bent to scratch him (wombats love being scratched along the back and behind the ears), and he grabbed my wrist and bit hard.

Blood spurted everywhere! I screamed and pulled away, and Rikki pulled even harder. *Hey, this is a great game,* he thought. *Let's wrestle!* The more I shrieked, the more he thought I was enjoying myself, and the more I pulled away, the more he tugged! Finally, I managed to get his jaws open. Rikki never had any idea he had hurt me. He thought we were both having fun.

A WOMBAT'S FUR

A wombat's skin is white, but its fur comes in different colors. Most Tasmanian wombats are gray. Some wombats, especially in very cold areas, go almost white in winter, then lose those coats in summer and turn brownish gray again. In our valley, wombats can be almost black or

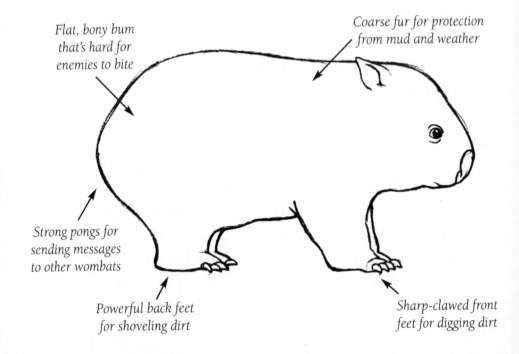

Flat, bony bum that's hard for enemies to bite

Coarse fur for protection from mud and weather

Strong pongs for sending messages to other wombats

Powerful back feet for shoveling dirt

Sharp-clawed front feet for digging dirt

deep brown or gray or even gold. Wombats usually go grayer as they get older; some just become paler and paler, so they are gold instead of brown. But I have known young wombats that were gray or gold.

Are there spotted wombats? No, you'll never see a spotted wombat, or a striped wombat, or even a wombat with pretty markings, as a horse or a cat might have. But dark wombats sometimes have patches of white fur. Smudge, for example, was gray except for a golden smudge across one ear and part of his head.

Wombat fur is very, very coarse—just like a doormat. If a wombat is out in light rain, only the top of its coat gets wet, so the wombat still stays warm. Even mud usually doesn't stick to wombat fur, though wombats can get pretty dusty.

A WOMBAT'S LEGS AND FEET

Wombats have short legs and fleshy pads on their feet, a bit like a dog's paws but broader, and they stand and walk in a very flat-footed manner. They don't stand on tiptoe like animals that run a lot.

The wombat's front feet have five long claws, and the more the wombat digs, the blunter and shorter the claws get. Some wombats have only tiny claws. Others, like our wombat Big Paws, never dig at all. His claws look as if he's been to a salon and had fake nails glued on.

A wombat's hind legs are longer and narrower than the front ones, with only four claws on each foot. The front feet dig; the back feet shovel out the dirt behind.

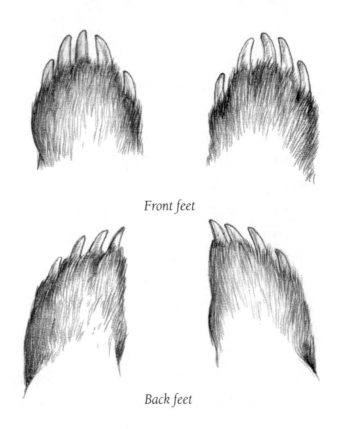

Front feet

Back feet

How fast can a wombat run? About twenty-five miles per hour. Wombats can't run that fast for very long, but they can put on a burst of speed over a short distance. I timed several of our wombats: Roadbat reached twenty miles per hour, and Burper hit over twenty-five. Gabby could only manage about six.

THE SEX OF A WOMBAT

How do you tell the difference between a male and a female wombat? The best way is to turn the wombat over. (*Warning:* Wombats will not like you checking them out. If you don't know what you're doing, you may lose a few fingers!)

Once a wombat is on its back, it's easy to see what sex it is. A male wombat has testicles. His penis is stored inside his body, so it doesn't dangle like those of many other mammals.

A female wombat has a pouch, but you may have to run your fingers through her fluffy tummy fur to find it. (Don't put your fingers into the pouch, though. If there's a tiny baby inside, you might hurt it.)

The pouch faces backward, with the opening between the female's back legs. That way it doesn't fill up with dirt

when she digs. Each pouch has two teats for the baby to drink from. The pouch itself is pink and nearly hairless, and there is a strong sphincter, or circular muscle, at the opening, which stops the very small wombat from falling out when the mother runs or jumps.

If you meet a wombat, and it growls at you, it's probably a female. I'm serious! A female wombat is often much stroppier than a male, especially if she has a baby. If the wombat has a baby bouncing after it, it's definitely a female. Look underneath the wombat, too. If there is a baby in the pouch, the pouch will sag. Sometimes the pouch sags even after the baby has left, so a droopy tummy indicates it's a female wombat.

The female wombat is usually a bit bigger than the male, but wombats vary so much in size that this way of telling them apart doesn't always work. The female often (but not always) has a narrower, pointier face than the male. As the male wombat grows older, his head tends to become wider and flatter.

4

A Day in the Life of a Wombat

Wombats go home to their burrows soon after sunrise, and that's where they spend most of the day. A wombat burrow is the perfect place for sleeping. No matter how hot or dry it is outside, inside the burrow the temperature and humidity remain comfortable.

Wombat holes usually have several bedrooms—chambers with soft, dry dust or a bed of dried grass or bracken on the floor. But some wombat burrows aren't deep enough to have rooms, so the wombat sleeps in a hollow just far enough underground to be sheltered from the sun. Sometimes the wombat scratches up its bed to make it fluffier or wriggles down into the dust. Then it sits on its bum and slowly falls asleep. Its eyes close. It sinks lower and lower until its head rests on the floor. Its body temperature begins to fall.

After an hour or more, the wombat rolls over onto its back, with its legs up in the air—the back legs straight up, and the front legs bent a bit. When a wombat is in this

position, it is very, *very* sound asleep. In fact, sometimes it's in such a deep sleep, it is impossible to wake!

SNEEZY

Sneezy lived in the wombat hole behind our bathroom. She's the only wombat I have ever known to get hay fever. Sometimes as I walked around the garden, I'd hear a sneeze deep underground. *Ah-choo!*

One morning I opened the back door. There was Sneezy, lying on her back on the doormat, her legs in the air. I prodded her with my foot. "Hey, wake up!" I said. "I want to go outside."

Sneezy didn't move.

I prodded her again. "Wake up, you dingbat wombat!"

Sneezy still didn't move. What was wrong?

I knelt down next to her. She didn't seem to be breathing! I couldn't feel a heartbeat, either, and her body seemed strangely stiff. I sat back. Had she died in the night? She'd been fine the evening before.

I cried a bit on the doorstep. Why had she died? Was there a wombat illness I didn't know of? Had her sneezing been a sign of lung disease?

By coincidence, a vet friend was coming for breakfast that morning. Maybe she could work out what had happened.

The vet and I lifted Sneezy up onto the kitchen table. She checked Sneezy over carefully, then shook her head. "I can't see anything wrong. It's a mystery," she said.

We dug a grave among the orange trees and carried Sneezy down. We lowered her into the grave . . . and she woke up! One very startled wombat blinked at us, then galloped for her hole behind the bathroom. A faint sound floated up from underground. *Ah-choo! Ah-choo!*

Sneezy wasn't dead! She'd been asleep. I'd had no idea, nor had the vet, that wombats could sleep so deeply. Most wombats don't sleep quite as soundly as Sneezy, but when they are in their deep-sleep stage, they can be very difficult to wake up.

A WOMBAT'S AFTERNOON

Usually wombats stay in their burrows until it gets dark. Too much heat or sunlight can kill a wombat. In fact, it can die of heat prostration within ten minutes on a hot sunny day. Sometimes wombats will sleep on their backs outside their holes on sunny afternoons in midwinter. But even then, if they spend too much time out in daylight, their skin dries out and they are more likely to get mange, a skin infection caused by tiny mites, which can leave them blind and deaf and in agony—or outright kill them.

During bad droughts, or if cattle and sheep have eaten all the grass, starving wombats desperate for food will come out during the day, hoping to get a bit more to eat. Sadly, those wombats don't live very long. Heat or mange kills them, or starvation. But if you live in a deep valley, as we do, you can watch wombats in the late afternoon from autumn to late spring. It's safe for wombats then. The sun goes behind the ridges, and the valley is in shadow.

Toward the end of the afternoon, the wombat wakes up in its bedchamber, moves closer to the entrance of the burrow, then goes to sleep again. But this time it isn't deeply asleep. It's just dozing and smelling the air, feeling the sun's warmth and waiting until it's cool and dark enough to go outside, and checking to see if there is any danger around. The hungrier the wombat is, the earlier it will venture out. If the weather is very cold or if it's raining hard, a wombat will stay in its burrow all night— sometimes even two nights in a row if it's a good growing season and the wombat is fat and not too hungry. But no matter what, it'll be out to feed the third night, even if the rain is still pouring down.

Then a wombat gets down to serious business: eating and scratching and leaving droppings. And for a wombat, these activities are very, very serious indeed.

⑤

Wombat Essentials

When you first see a wombat, it will probably be either eating or scratching. Sometimes it will be eating *and* scratching. That's how you can tell if a wombat is outside at night—you'll hear a steady *chomp, chomp, chomp* interrupted by, or along with, *scratch, scratch, scratch*.

WHAT WOMBATS LIKE TO EAT

If wombats were given the choice of every wonderful food in the universe, they'd choose grass—lovely lush green

grass. When there isn't a lot of soft grass about, wombats eat many other things. Wombats have long, strong teeth, so they can chew up tough sedges and tussocks. They'll eat the bark from young trees and dig up all sorts of roots. They'll often have a nibble, too, of other things they find: mushrooms, moss on a rock, a fallen avocado. But usually it's the younger wombats who experiment with new tastes. The older ones stick to what they know, unless they're very hungry.

RIKKI AND HIS MATES

I mentioned Rikki the Wrestler earlier. He went bush—returned to the wild—as wombats do when they reach a certain age. Then a drought hit, and it got drier and drier . . . and one afternoon there was an *aaark!* at the back door. (*Aaark!* is wombat for "Feed me now, or I'll bash your door down!")

It was Rikki, and he had four unfamiliar wombats with him. I put some oats in a dish for him—really, an old hubcap nailed to a big piece of wood so that he couldn't knock it over. Then I put down food for the other wombats, too. They looked a bit uneasy, as though they weren't quite sure about dropping in on a human for dinner. But they ate the oats.

Every afternoon after that there were five wombats waiting for their dinner. Then there were six . . . then seven. Luckily, it finally rained, or we might have been feeding a hundred wombats.

Rikki and his mates went bush as soon as the grass grew, and we never saw any of them again. But I was always glad that he'd been able to say to them, "Hey, come on. I know where there's some pretty good tucker!"

Wombats living in different areas will eat different foods—and sometimes wombats in the same area will have different favorites. If wombats have been reared by people, they'll have been introduced to a variety of things, like carrots, sweet potatoes, corn on the cob, rolled oats, and wombat nuts (a biscuit-like treat made of grain and alfalfa).

Just like people, wombats can be fussy eaters. I've raised wombats that wouldn't touch a carrot, while others would break the door down to get more of them. Wombats that live in orchards often learn to like fruit. We grow 130 different kinds of apples, so there are ripe apples from November (our spring) to July (midwinter). A wombat we call Grunter spends his nights eating windfall apples and pears. (We call him that because all those apples make him burp—and fart—and "Grunter" is a more polite name than "Farter.")

SMUDGE AND THE APRICOTS

Smudge, the first wombat I lived with, loved apricots. He sat under the apricot tree waiting for ripe fruit to fall. He munched them carefully, eating around the pits. His fur grew sticky, and his droppings were squishy and smelled like rotten apricot.

The first summer I knew him, I decided to dry some

apricots. I picked six cases of them, then cut each apricot in half and laid them out on sheets of aluminum foil to dry in the sun. Every night I took them inside, so they wouldn't get wet in the dew; then every morning I spread them out again. One afternoon I came back late from town and raced up the hill to take the apricots inside.

And then I stopped and stared.

There were no apricots to be seen. But there was a very stuffed wombat, sitting by the foil with his eyes half closed. Every now and then he let out a burp that smelled of apricot.

I didn't see Smudge for two nights after that. And he was never interested in apricots again.

Wombats that are hungry—or have grown up during a drought or in an area where there isn't a lot of good food around—look as if they're vacuuming the grass as they eat. They stand with their heads down, munching steadily. Wombats eating during lush periods are much fussier. They nose about for things that they *really* like to eat.

If there is a big sweet patch of grass or a bowl of wombat nuts, they will sit on their bums to eat. But usually they eat standing on all fours. They'll travel a long way to find their favorite foods—they'll even dig through snow to find food.

DO WOMBATS DRINK?

Young wombats drink milk from their mothers. Adult wombats drink water, but in lush periods they may get enough moisture from grass and dew. Like most nocturnal animals, wombats prefer to drink at dusk, soon after they wake up, and they drink very, very slowly.

Wombats usually take the same path to water and drink at the same place. But if there is a strange scent around, like a dog's, they may avoid that drinking spot for days. Wombats that are more familiar with dog smell seem less worried by a reasonably old scent.

HOW TO SCRATCH A WOMBAT

Wombats love to scratch themselves. They'll often rub up against a post or a tree to leave their scent, as cats do.

But mostly they scratch because
they're itchy. They'll scratch with
their front legs or their back legs.
They'll sneak beneath parked cars
and scratch their backs on the cars'
undersides—and get very greasy in
the process. They'll rub their backs
on garden chairs and tables, usually knocking them over. We have
an earthquake every morning at
about two o'clock. It's really Mothball. She has wandered out of her
burrow and across her "veranda"
so she can scratch her back on
the floor joist below our bed. One
small wombat is quite strong
enough to shake the floor and rat-
tle the books next to the bed.

A wombat will stop whatever it's doing to have a
scratch. It may be eating steadily, or bashing down a door,
or pushing its way through a fence. But suddenly it will
stop, as if it can think of only one thing at a time—and at
that precise moment, it's an itch!

Wombats don't lick or groom themselves the way cats
and other animals do. But sometimes a female wombat
will sit on her bum and lean over to lick and groom her
pouch area, or scratch it gently, or wriggle her tummy on
damp grass.

A wombat that's familiar with humans loves to be scratched, especially behind its ears or on the bony ridge along its back—a place it can't quite reach by itself. The harder you scratch, the better the wombat likes it, especially if you rub your boot along its back. Often it will go all weak in the knees and flop down into doormat position, with a look of wombat bliss on its face. A wombat will also lie on its back to be scratched, though you have to be gentler when it's in this position.

A WOMBAT IS NOT . . .

A bear.
Although it looks a bit like one.

A badger.
They both live in holes and are hairy, but that's about it.

Allowed on the sofa.
This means you, Mothball—off!

A pet.
Wombats will always be wild animals. They may bite you or growl at you. They need the freedom to wander, to dig, and to have their own wombat lives to be really happy. Wombats that become fond of humans may look for humans . . . and die as they run after cars or dogs or hunters.

6

Wombats and Friends

Wombats don't seem to make friends with each other the way dogs—and people—do. A baby wombat will live with its mother until it is grown. Otherwise, wombats live alone. Each has a favorite burrow, but it will also have other burrows it visits regularly. Burrows may be used by more than one wombat—just not at the same time. A wombat will sniff to find out if there's another wombat inside—and turn away if there is. But if it is scared, it will charge right in. Then you'll hear *grg! chomp!* as the wombat that's already there tries to bite the visitor's nose. Both wombats will race out to fight properly. But if there is a dog outside, or a fox or a human they're scared of, they'll both dash inside again, and this time the first wombat will let the other one stay there, safe from danger.

DO WOMBATS SHARE?

A wombat doesn't have a territory the way some animals do. It has an area where it feeds most of the time, and

*Mothers will share grass with their babies,
but other wombats have to keep their distance.*

other wombats can share this space as long as they stay two or three yards away. Sometimes several wombats will eat at the same time, but usually one will feed at one time, then another will feed later that night.

Young, fit wombats usually take the best feeding times: early evening and just before dawn. An old, sick wombat may feed in a good grassy area only when other wombats don't want to, such as in the late afternoon, when it's still too hot to be comfortable.

Wombats are often more tolerant of each other when there's a drought and not much grass—or, conversely, when it has rained and there's so much grass that an army of wombats, kangaroos, and wallabies couldn't eat it all. But some wombats jealously guard "their" grass and won't let any other animal near, no matter what the circumstances. I have seen Mothball bite a wallaby on the leg because it dared to eat where she was feeding. Then she chased it right down to the orchard!

DO WOMBATS TALK?

Wombats know each other by smell and by the smell of their scat, or droppings. They mostly don't use sounds to communicate. And they don't learn *our* words, the way dogs do. I have never known a wombat to learn its name—or, at least, the name I've given it.

The wild wombats that live near us don't pay any attention when I call them. They only come for food when they can smell it. Baby wombats that are brought up with humans will learn that when a person yells, there might be food around. But they don't care what words you use. You can yell "Here, wombat!" or "There's a dead mouse in the sink!" and they'll come just the same.

Wombats *do* make a few sounds that you can learn to recognize. *Gnug, gnug, gnug* means "Here I am. Where are you?" Baby wombats make this sound if their mothers are too far away. *Yip* with a snarl can mean "This is *my* territory—get lost!" or "Feed me my carrots immediately!" Or it might just mean "Me, wombat! Obey!" *Growlllarf!* means "Get away at once!" If a mother wombat makes this sound when you are near her baby—run!

Sometimes a wombat meets another wombat as they wander through the bush, and they stop, nose to nose.

They may stay like that for ten minutes or half an hour. I have no idea what they are doing. Gossiping? Exchanging smells? If only my nose were as good as a wombat's, I could "talk" to them and find out.

WOMBAT FIGHTS: BUM BITING AND BATTLES

Most wombats snarl but don't attack. But wombats *can* be vicious fighters. If one wombat wants another wombat to go away, it growls. If growling doesn't work, it gives a high-pitched yell. And if yelling fails, it sneaks up behind the second wombat and bites it on the bum. The bitten wombat then lunges around and tries to bite the first wombat.

Usually, the wombat that yells the most wins. It doesn't matter how big a wombat is or how long its teeth are. The top wombat is the one who is stroppiest and growls longest and loudest. The other wombat just runs off, as though it doesn't think it's worth arguing. But sometimes wombat confrontations turn into real fights.

It's hard to attack something that is mostly bone and muscle and tough skin. A fighting wombat will try to tear off an opponent's ear, bite it on the nose, or—if the opponent is a male—rip off its testicles. Any part that can be grabbed and torn is vulnerable. But usually one wombat retreats before either is badly hurt.

Wombats are most likely to be hurt when they attack each other inside burrows. They can't turn around in a narrow hole to present their tough bums to their opponents, so their noses or ears can get badly bitten.

Sometimes wombats just plain hate each other. They'll yell at each other every night until one of them decides to leave the area. But mostly they just avoid the wombats they don't get along with.

MORIARTY

The stroppiest wombat I ever knew was Moriarty. She was small (a bit like a soccer ball with legs—and teeth), but she never let any other animal near her feeding area. Moriarty attacked wombats, wallabies, echidnas, and a king parrot that was silly enough to land beside her nose. She attacked everything, including me.

It was my fault. I decided to fence the vegetable garden—mostly to stop the wallabys from eating my corn and carrots. But Moriarty's bum was parked exactly where the gate was going to go.

"Hey, you!" I said. "Move!"

Moriarty kept eating.

"Go away, you dingbat wombat!" I yelled.

Eeeegh! snarled Moriarty. She grabbed my boot between her jaws and bit down hard. Luckily, my boots were tough.

"Sorry about this, wombat," I said. Then I turned the hose on her.

Moriarty bit at the water but found nothing to sink her fangs into. She shot me a damp, disgusted look, then dashed for the thorn bush. She peered out, angry and bedraggled. *Eeeegh!* she complained.

From then on it was war.

I finished the fence that afternoon, and Moriarty was locked out of the vegetable garden . . . for about ten minutes.

Moriarty dug under the wire.

I weighed the wire down with rocks.

Moriarty burrowed under the rocks.

I buried the wire a foot and a half deep.

Moriarty burrowed under the wire.

I filled in her burrow with more rocks.

Moriarty dug the rocks out.

Then I asked a friend to help me move in a truckload of giant boulders.

"There's no way a wombat can move these!" declared my friend. But the next morning the boulders had been shifted, and Moriarty was in the vegetable garden . . . again.

How could one small wombat move such heavy rocks?

That night I stayed up late to keep watch. There was no sign of Moriarty. I stayed up late the second night, too. Still no wombat. But on the third night, a small round brown shape padded down to the vegetable garden.

Was that something in her mouth? I peered into the moonlight. It was a tomato stake. Even now it's hard to believe what I saw that night: Moriarty using that tomato stake as a lever! The rock moved one inch, two . . . just enough for a furry body to squeeze past.

I've never again seen a wombat use a tool, though I *did* see Mothball move a box so she could stand on it to attack the mop!

I gave up on fencing the garden after that. I started another vegetable garden beyond the creek. Moriarty had won the war.

She died seven years later, in the old vegetable garden, gray and thin and crusted with scabs from mange. A slow death from age and mange is not something you'd wish on anyone. But even as she died, she glared at me, daring me to try to help her. She would have used her last breath to bite me, I'm sure.

She's buried where she died.

After she was gone, a black-tailed wallaby began grazing in the old vegetable garden, munching with glee the young oats springing up from the mulch. I wondered how long he'd been waiting, looking longingly at the feast, intimidated by Moriarty, the meanest wombat I have ever known.

7

Wombats Growing Up

When a wombat is a baby, it is the cuddliest, most playful creature in the universe. In our valley, baby wombats are mostly born in January or February, and they come out of their mothers' pouches in late August or early September.

A WOMBAT'S FIRST YEAR

A human baby spends about nine months in its mother's womb before it is born. A wombat baby emerges from its mother's womb after only twenty days! A tiny hairless pink blob, it crawls up her fur to her pouch, attaches itself to one of her two teats, and starts sucking.

At three to four months, the baby wombat weighs between eight and nine ounces and is still attached to its mother's teat. It has fur on its ears, and you can make out its nose and mouth. The mum's pouch is bigger now. She sometimes growls at other wombats if they come too close. If she dies when the baby is this young, and if

Wombat, age 3–4 months,
attached to its mother's teat

Wombat, age 6–7 months,
leaving its mother's pouch

expert human caretakers then look after the baby, it may survive. But it will need a lot of love and care.

At six months, the baby starts moving about the pouch. Its body is still pink, and its nose and feet are an even brighter pink. Sometimes, it peers out of the pouch, but all you really see is a bright pink nose peeping from between its mum's legs.

When the baby is seven to eight months old, its mother's pouch droops close to the ground. The baby gets out of the pouch in the burrow. But it still stays very close to Mum. It sleeps on top of her head or draped over her body or next to her. When she goes out to graze, the baby goes along in her pouch and puts its head out between her back legs and has a taste of grass, too. Then it does a somersault and pokes its back legs out to urinate. The baby is now quite large: six to seven pounds. It drinks a lot of milk, so it produces a lot of urine!

At nine to ten months, the baby spends nearly all of its time out of the pouch. Its nose is still pink, though not as bright as before, but the soles of its feet are darker and its fur is darkening, too. It's a brown wombat now, not a pink one. It still drinks milk from its mother, but mostly it doesn't bother to get all the way into the pouch when it wants a snack. It leaves its own droppings now but usually hides them under a bush.

The baby is still scared of strange noises. If frightened, it darts back to the burrow or to Mum. But this is a very playful time. The baby is still well fed with milk, so it doesn't need to graze as steadily as its mother. It has lots of time and energy to bounce at shadows, leap out at passing wallabies, or sniff how the universe smells. This is the time when a baby wombat will sometimes play with people. It wants to play with *someone,* and Mum is usually too busy eating.

PLAYING GAMES WITH WOMBATS

The first wombat baby I ever played with was Sneezy's baby Lurk. I woke up one day to a din. *Clang, clang, banga, banga, clang, crash, whomp!* Was the house falling down? I looked outside. It was Lurk, on the patio.

Clanga, clanga, clanga! Lurk, bashed the screen door to set it swinging. *Banga, banga, banga!* Lurk jumped on the bouncenette seat and got it clattering. *Whomp, whomp, whomp!* Lurk attacked the rocking chair, then raced back to bash the door again before it stopped swinging.

"Hoy!" I yelled.

Lurk gave a bounce as though to say, "Come on! Let's play!"

"No way," I said. "I'm going back to bed."

But I did play with him a few nights later. I wandered down to the orange trees in the moonlight to pick some fruit for breakfast. Suddenly, something hit my knees from behind, almost knocking me down.

It was Lurk.

"What's going on?" I demanded, and then I realized: Lurk wanted to play.

It was a simple game. Lurk hid behind a bush and jumped out at me; then I hid behind a bush and jumped out at him. Wombats are much better at jumping out at humans than humans are at jumping out at wombats. But we played the hide-and-seek game often after that, dancing at each other in the moonlight. I have played it with other wombats since.

GROWING UP

At twelve to fifteen months, the baby stops drinking milk, but how this happens varies a lot. Sometimes it just stops; other times it may drink every few days or still want to drink, but the mother discourages it by lying flat on the ground or by giving it a nip. The baby will start roaming farther away from Mum and the burrow. It may start marking territory, leaving tiny soft droppings around the house, on the stairs, or on rocks. Or it may still hide its scat, so a bigger adult wombat won't try to chase it away.

By eighteen months, the young wombat looks much like an adult, although it will keep growing for about another year. Its face is more finely featured, with a proportionally longer nose and softer whiskers than an adult's, and its bum isn't as rounded as it will be when it's fully grown. At this point, Mum may take off, leaving junior behind . . . or junior may wander off . . . or Mum may take junior for a long walk and come home without him.

Most young wombats dig a bit at this age, but they

rarely make a complete burrow—or one that holds up. Still, any freshly dug dirt will attract them, and they love tearing off bits of shrubbery, too.

At two years old, the young wombat is independent. It might wander far off into a new territory, but more often, at least where I live, it will stay close by, and its territory will overlap its mother's. This depends on the season. In good years, young wombats are more likely to roam farther afield. In bad years, all wombats stay close to the best feeding grounds.

At two to three years, the wombat is an adult. It marks its territory with its scent and its droppings, and it uses them to communicate in other ways, too. It is about this time that it starts to mate.

WOMBATS MATING

Once a year, female wombats "go into heat." This is the only time when they are able to become pregnant if they mate, and it lasts only a few days.

A female wombat in heat will leave oily drops along with her scat, and the oily stuff may also be dropped as she walks, or rubbed on tussocks or rocks or trees. The drops are very, very stinky. Even *I* can smell them from about 30 yards away, so wombats can probably smell them from miles away!

A male wombat will chase a female for about three days before she agrees to mate, both of them yelling and shrieking as they run. For years I thought the females were try-

ing to run away, but then I saw Flat White, one of the female wombats in our garden, yip at Big Paws, to get him to
chase her. (He wasn't interested.) If the male catches the female during this time, he might bite her—or she might
bite him, or chase him, too, though this doesn't happen as
often.

For the first couple of days, it looks as though the
wombats are really angry with each other. But on the last
day, they behave more as if they're playing. They nip and
chase each other; then the female darts into her burrow,
the male follows her, and they mate. Once they're done,
the male comes out and starts to feed. So does the female,
and they ignore each other from then on.

Around our region, many wombats have a baby about
once every three years. But some only ever have one,

while others—like Two-and-a-Half—have a new baby nearly every year. For a long time people thought that a drought or a lush year didn't have any effect on breeding; there were as many babies in pouches in droughts as there were in lush years. But in the last six years our area has experienced the worst drought ever recorded, and there were no baby wombats at all in this end of the valley. Then last February I heard the wombats mating again, and I knew it was going to rain.

It did. We've had the wettest spring and summer in decades—and there are baby wombats everywhere. It seems that there's still an enormous lot to learn about wombats. (And if you want a good long-range weather forecast, ask a wombat.)

Most wombats don't go into heat again until their babies have left home completely, though this isn't always the case. Two-and-a-Half sometimes had a baby in her pouch *and* a baby bouncing beside her.

A STUBBORN BABY WOMBAT

Sometimes a baby wombat doesn't want to leave the pouch, even when it's too big to fit inside. Hark, Mothball's baby, was like that. So for a while we had a two-headed wombat. At one end was Mothball's head, eating grass. And at the other end was Hark's head, poking out between Mothball's back legs and eating grass, too.

Finally, Mothball worked out how to get her stubborn baby out of her pouch. As I watched from my study window one afternoon, she trotted up to the herb garden with a determined look on her face. She leapt at the garden wall. *Whump!* Her pouch bashed against the stones. She leapt at the wall again. *Whump!*

Hark poked his head out of the pouch. He looked slightly stunned.

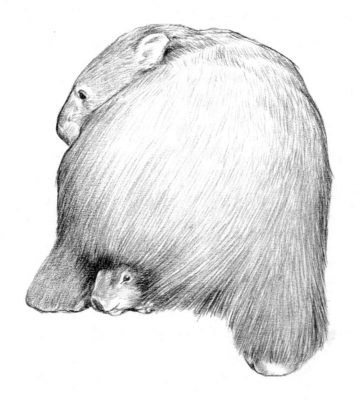

Mothball leapt a third time. *Whump!*

That was it! Hark crawled out of the pouch. He gazed around nervously, as though to say, "This world is big!"

Mothball ignored him. She began to eat grass. A few

minutes later Hark began to eat, too. Ten minutes later he decided that it was time for a nap. He started to stick his head back in his mum's pouch, and . . . *Thud!* Mothball flopped flat on the grass on her tummy. Hark tried to wriggle under her, to get back in. But Mothball wasn't moving.

Finally, Hark decided that the big wild world wasn't as terrifying as he'd thought, and he started to eat grass. He and his mum were still munching grass together when I went out to pick some beans for dinner. I bent down and began to hunt through the bean bushes. *Whump!* Something dived headfirst down my sweater. It did a somersault. Then a small brown face peered up at me as though to say, "Aha! A big wombat pouch!" (Never lean over when there's a baby wombat about!)

For a while Hark followed Mothball's heels. Then one afternoon I looked out to see her padding determinedly up the mountain with Hark at her side. It seemed she had decided that it was time he was weaned. Two days later she was back, but there was no sign of Hark. He did return a year later, though. He and Mothball don't have much to do with each other now. They just sniff each other vaguely as they pass, as though to say, "Hey, I knew you once, didn't I?"

⑧

Wombat Burrows

Nearly all young wombats start to dig a few holes, and nearly all wombats do lots of digging to renovate the old burrows they move into. Wombats also dig to mark their territory or because they're angry or just because the fresh dirt smells good. Humans may sing if they're happy or sad or bored. Wombats dig!

Wombats are great diggers, but most of them are *lousy* engineers. In all the time I've studied wombats, I've seen

only one—Mothball—dig a new burrow that didn't collapse, and even that hole filled up with water whenever it rained.

Most wombats renovate old burrows. A wombat moves into a hole that hasn't been used for months or years. It clears out any dirt that has fallen into the passages. Then it hauls in new bracken or tussocks to make a bed.

This means that wombats live in burrows that were dug ten, fifty, one hundred years ago—or, who knows, maybe thousands of years ago. It also means that if wombats are going to move into an area, there have to be wombat holes already there for them to shelter in. If the old holes have been destroyed by farming or logging, and there aren't any wombats about that are good engineers, there won't be any burrows for them to move into.

The soil has to be right for a wombat burrow, too. Heavy soil that can be compacted into hard walls is best, with rocks or tree roots to help support the entrance. You can't dig a good burrow in sand!

INSIDE A WOMBAT BURROW

Wombat burrows are fascinating! There are passages that go deep into the hill, and rooms that are large enough for a person to sit up in.

When I was younger—and thinner—I used to wriggle down wombat holes. These days, zoologists can put miniature trackers or cameras on wombats to see what happens deep underground. But years ago the only way I knew how to explore was to crawl down inside on my tummy. I was nervous the first time I did it. I wondered: Will I get stuck and never be able to get out? Will I meet a snake? What if the hole collapses? What if I can't turn around?

But it wasn't like that at all. As soon as I got inside, the passageway dipped down, then up again. Then it opened into a tiny room. I could sit up and shine my torch around. The walls were hard, and the floor was soft, fine dust. At one end of the room was an opening to another tunnel. I lay on my tummy and started wriggling again.

After a yard or so, I came to another room. This one was even bigger. And it had a bed made of a pile of dry bracken and tussocks. The burrow became narrower after that, so I didn't go any farther. But the other wombat burrows I have been down were much the same: passageways, then rooms. Sometimes there would be a tunnel off to one side, occasionally with old wombat bones in it.

The deepest wombat burrows located in our valley go hundreds of yards into the hillsides and have lots of entrances. Others in sheltered spots, like the one Mothball lives in under our bedroom, are only six or seven feet long.

DIFFERENT TYPES OF BURROWS

The perfect wombat burrow has a narrow entrance, to discourage dogs and foxes. The passageway dips down and

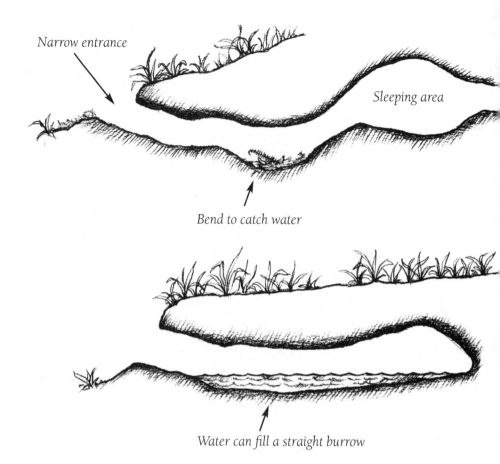

Narrow entrance

Sleeping area

Bend to catch water

Water can fill a straight burrow

then rises up again, so rainwater can't pool in the main room. Badly engineered burrows just go straight in, so when it rains, water rushes down into them. Often they collapse. The perfect wombat burrow has great big rooms with soft, dry sand and several openings, so that the wombat can travel safely underground and escape if there is danger. But you rarely find the perfect wombat burrow, just as you rarely find the perfect house!

Most wombats are conservative. They like traditional wombat burrows. But once when Bryan and I were exploring some caves, we came upon a very startled wombat. This wombat had made the caves her home. Some of them were big enough for us to stand up in—a wombat mansion!

Roadbat used to live in the drainage pipes under the road. Of course, every time it rained, the pipes filled up with mud, and he had to dig them out again. But they were cool and sheltered him from the sun—what more did he need?

HOW WOMBATS GET THEIR OWN BURROWS

When a young wombat wants a burrow of its own, it looks for an empty one—one where the former resident has died or moved out. Most wombats die deep underground, so the new wombat scratches out all the bones and any old bedding or bits of collapsed ceiling. It carries in new bracken or grass for its bed. Then it leaves its droppings all about outside, so that other wombats know that the burrow is now occupied.

Sometimes a really stroppy newcomer will take over another wombat's burrow, either by snarling and yelling or by fighting a real battle. But most wombats don't like to fight. If a stroppy wombat demands a burrow, then the other wombat just leaves.

Sometimes a wombat will dig a new front door for an old hole. I wandered down to one of our paddocks one day and found a great pile of dirt and a new entrance to a giant wombat burrow that I'd never guessed was under my feet. There hadn't been a wombat in that burrow for at least thirty years, and maybe a lot longer. Horses and cattle—with their large heavy bodies and small hard hooves—had destroyed the old entrance long before. But somehow a new wombat had worked out that somewhere down there was a palace.

A BURROW IN A TREE

Wombats live in holes in the ground. Koalas live in trees. But once I found a wombat burrow in a tree. It was a giant dead tree. It had been hit by lightning years earlier, and the top had broken off. The wombat hole started under the roots, then wound up the inside of the tree trunk. The wombat had dug away the old wood as if it were dirt. The hole ended at the top, about twenty feet up, where the wombat had leveled off a platform to sit on and to look out over the valley.

But wombats are short-sighted—they can't see very far. So why on earth would a wombat want to look out over the valley? It took me years to work it out: It was smelling the view, not looking at it.

9

Wombat Intelligence

Wombats are different from people, and not just because they are furry and walk on four legs. They see the world in a different way from human beings—and from dogs and other animals, too. Their intelligence is different from ours as well.

HOW WOMBATS SEE THE WORLD

We usually learn about the world by processing what we see or hear. Wombats learn about the world by the way it smells. A wombat would be a hundred times better as a tracker than a dog, and a thousand times better than a human—if anyone could ever train a wombat!

Wombats sit on a hill and "see" the view by smelling it. When we look at a view, we see only what it looks like *now*. But when a wombat smells a view, it can smell what was happening yesterday . . . and the day before . . . and maybe even weeks ago.

HOW WOMBATS HEAR THE WORLD

Wombats have very good hearing, but they're not good at processing the information they hear. They have to think awhile to understand what they've heard, just as we sometimes have to think for a few seconds to work out what we've smelled. If a wombat hears a car, it thinks, *Do I hear something? Yes, I do. What is it? Oh, yes . . . it's a car. I'd better run.* But by that time, it may be too late. That's why so many wombats are run over; they literally run under cars, because they have only just worked out that they're in danger.

HOW SMART ARE WOMBATS?

Wombats are quite smart, but their sort of intelligence is different from ours. One of the common ways to test animals for intelligence and memory is to put them in a maze and measure how long it takes them to find their way to food or freedom, and then measure how accurately they remember the maze on subsequent attempts.

If you put a rat (or a dog or a person) in a maze, it will race around, working out how to get out. A wombat will either just sit there or try to bash the walls down. So a person looking at the wombat might think, *Dumb animal.* But it's not. When you're built like a small hairy tank, it makes sense to sit still if there is danger or to try to crash through it. I suspect that if a wombat had a chance to *smell* its way out of the maze, it would be a champion.

THE CLEVEREST WOMBAT OF ALL

Wombats can learn, but you can't teach them anything; they absorb only the information *they* find useful. However, wombats can learn to count. I first tested this with a wombat we cared for named Pudge. She was the most intelligent wombat I have known.

Pudge expected two carrots every night. But one night I had only one carrot left. Pudge ate it—then bashed up the garbage bin for half an hour after she realized that no more carrots were coming out the back door.

The second night, I decided to see what she'd do if I cut one carrot in two. Pudge ate both halves . . . and didn't bash the garbage bin. It was the "two" that mattered, not the amount of carrot. So I wondered: How many carrots could Pudge count?

Each night for the next week, I cut her carrot into three pieces. Then one night I gave her two whole carrots, instead of one carrot cut into three. *Aaark!* Pudge attacked the garbage bin until I put out her rightful carrot ration again.

Finally, Pudge was counting six bits of carrot—and yelling if I only put out five. But by that time, she was wandering off regularly, so I was never able to figure out exactly how many she could count up to.

Maybe wombats can count to ten . . . or twenty . . . or thirty. Perhaps wombats could do algebra if they thought there was a carrot in it for them. Or maybe I just had a genius wombat, and no other wombat can even count to two. I still haven't found out.

10

Wombat Communication

Wombats "talk" to each other with their droppings and other smells. Wherever you go in wombat territory, you'll see wombat scat.

Small wombats leave small droppings, usually pointed at one end. Large wombats leave giant ones—the bigger the wombat, the bigger the scat. A wombat can leave a hundred droppings a night.

Wombat scat doesn't pong, even if you pick one up and sniff it. Wombats mostly eat grass, so their droppings smell like grass, too—just a bit digested.

In a drought, when there isn't much grass or the grass is tough and brown, wombat droppings are dark brown to black and shaped like squares, sometimes joined together like building blocks. This is a great shape if you want your droppings to stay on a rock. (Round scat would fall off.) When the grass is lush, wombat droppings are green and slightly sloppy, and they are dropped wherever the wombat happens to be. Most of the time, though, wombats are very deliberate about where they leave their scat.

WHERE DO WOMBATS LEAVE THEIR DROPPINGS?

Many droppings will be placed on the highest point around, especially if the wombat is female. If male wombats come across scat placed on the ground, they often make long scrapes next to it. Sometimes females do this, too, especially if there are strange wombats about that they have been trying to chase off.

Wombats also leave droppings on any newly dug dirt. I have no idea if this is to say, "Hey, this dirt is mine!" or "Hey, nice smell!" And any new thing in a wombat's territory will probably have scat placed on it overnight. If Bryan makes a new rock garden, it's decorated the next morning with a large pile of wombat droppings. Fallen branches, new shoes outside the back door, a new door-

When the grass is dry and brown, droppings are brown and squarish.

When the grass is lush, droppings are softer and joined together.

Baby wombat droppings are small and pointed.

mat—all will be greeted with not just one dropping but a neat pile.

The droppings aren't just territory markers. Each pile carries information: which wombat left it, the wombat's hormonal and emotional state, how old it is, and possibly—probably—many other things that I just don't have sufficient wombat intelligence to work out.

OTHER WOMBAT SMELLS

Wombats pong. (Dogs find me a very interesting person to sniff; I always have a faint wombat smell on my shoes and clothes.) Wombats learn a lot about each other from the way their droppings smell. But their other pongs say a lot, too. Many animals produce pheromones—special scents. A wombat's smell probably tells another wombat many things, including if a female is in heat.

11

How to Meet a Wombat

People who see wombats in zoos see bored, sleepy animals with too little room to do all the interesting things wombats do in the wild. If you really want to meet wombats playing wombat games and leading real wombat lives, you have to travel to Australia, you have to go bush, and you have to watch for them at night or in late afternoon on winter days.

HOW TO FIND A WOMBAT IN THE BUSH

1. Look for droppings.
If there are wombats about, you'll soon see scat on the highest, most obvious, spot a wombat can reach with its bum.
2. Sniff out wombat odors.
Once you know what a wombat smells like, the pong is unmistakable!
3. Look for wombat scratches.
Wombats will scratch in fresh dirt or places where they've left their droppings.

4. Look for wombat burrows.

This isn't the best way to tell if there's a wombat about, because the burrow may have been empty for years. Look around the entrance for freshly dug earth, paw prints, scratches, and droppings. If you're not sure there's a wombat inside, neatly rake the dirt in front of the hole. Look for prints the next day. If there are big and small prints, a mother and baby may live in the burrow.

5. Look for wombat "sits."

Wombats often have spots—high on a ridge or hill— where they sit to smell a view. The ground at these "sits" will be worn bare by the wombats' bums. You won't see droppings there, but you'll find them nearby.

6. Look for dust or sand baths.

Old wombats love to roll in warm dust on winter days— I think it helps ease their aches and pains. (Wombats can get arthritis.) During hot, dry periods, wombats also dig baths in wet sand to cool themselves down or soothe the itch from mange.

7. Look for wombat tracks.

A wombat's front paw print looks a bit like a dog's paw print, while its back paw print looks a bit like a very small human footprint. You'll find wombat tracks in sand by creeks, in soft dirt, and beside wombat burrows. The prints will tell you if the wombat has been ambling along, standing to eat, crouching to drink, or running away from danger. When a wombat is trudging along normally, the

Dog's paw print   Wombat's front paw print

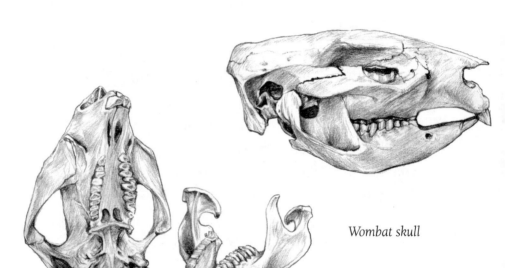

Wombat skull

front and back prints are close together. When it is running, they are farther apart.

8. Look for wombat bones.

Most wombats die in their burrows, but a few years later the burrow will be cleaned out by the next wombat resident. Dogs, foxes, and monitor lizards may also drag the bones out. You can recognize a wombat skull by the two long front teeth in the upper and lower jaws, with smaller teeth much farther back.

9. Listen for wombat noises.

Wombats are noisy eaters. You'll hear them going *chomp, chomp, chomp!* They're also noisy scratchers, and they scratch themselves often. You'll also hear grunts, huffs, snarls, and yips if they are mating, and sometimes burps, farts, sneezes, coughs, and other noises.

10. Keep watch in the same spot.

Wombats like familiar smells and have favorite patches of grass. They're also creatures of habit. If a wombat comes to a certain pool to drink at dusk or to a particular patch of grass to eat at one o'clock in the morning, or if it uses a special branch to scratch, you'll probably find it there the next night—or even the next month.

WHY YOU SHOULD SING TO WOMBATS

Years ago I accidentally discovered how to get really close to wombats without scaring them away. I was living in the shed in the bush at the time, mostly by myself. And because there was no one around to yell "Shut up!" I sang as I worked in the orchards. I noticed that if I walked through the bush, the wombats ran away as soon as I came close, but if I *sang* and walked slowly, they just went on eating. I could come right up to them or sit and watch what they were doing.

Why? Well, wombats aren't afraid of humans, but they're very easily startled. If you yell, "Hey! There's a wombat!" and run up to it, it will race away in shock. But if you stand still and let it smell you, the wombat will slowly come closer to investigate—or just ignore you and go about its business. And if you sing to a wombat, it will know where you are and won't be startled by your presence.

It doesn't matter what you sing or how well. You just need to keep singing—softly. I know it sounds weird, but it works. And it's how I've been able to spy on the wombats for so long.

Other music doesn't work, so don't try bringing in a rock band. Wombats mostly don't enjoy music or even notice it. They just like it when you sing because then they know exactly where you are and what you're doing. And if you really hate singing, recite poetry instead—in a soothing voice.

(12)

Caring for Orphan Wombats

Even if a mother wombat has been killed by a car or by a dog or has been shot, the baby in her pouch might still be alive. Sometimes baby wombats are rescued and brought to people like me who have been trained to look after injured wild animals.

Looking after a baby wombat is an enormous amount of work and responsibility. The baby must be fed every two hours and kept warm and clean. The experience can also be heartbreaking, as an orphan wombat may have been hurt when its mother was killed, and it will be in shock and can very easily die.

But a baby wombat is a wonderful, cuddly animal and is fascinating to live with—if you don't mind wombat droppings in your closet or chewed-up toilet paper in the bathroom. Above all, it is an incredible privilege to share your life for a while with a wild animal.

Here are some of the absolute essentials I have learned about caring for baby wombats.

1. Milk requirements

A baby wombat needs between 10 and 15 percent of its body weight in milk every day. This must be low-lactose milk or milk especially formulated for marsupials. Never feed a wombat cow's milk in any form at all, or vitamins, or anything with sugar or salt in it. If you're not sure that the baby is getting enough milk, you have to weigh it to check that it is putting on weight, just as you would a human baby.

2. Feeding requirements

A baby wombat needs to be fed every two hours until its fur grows in, and every three hours after that, right through the night. Wombats are nocturnal, and a baby may go to sleep on you during the day, so coaxing it to drink enough milk can take up a lot of your time.

Most baby wombats prefer to feed while lying on their backs, which is the way wombats feed in the pouch. But I have known one wombat that demanded to be on its stomach.

Never force-feed a wombat. Just keep cuddling it and offering it milk until it finds the smell and taste familiar enough to try a little. If the wombat wants to be fed, feed it.

3. General care

After every feeding, clean around the baby's mouth with a damp cloth to make sure there is no dried milk caking its lips or chin. When the bedding is soiled, change it. There is a delicate balance between hygiene and keeping a nice familiar wombat smell to reassure the baby.

If the baby doesn't have fur, wipe its body every day with lanolin and make sure its bedding is very soft. When the baby is fully furred, though still pink rather than brown (about eight months old), let it play on fresh green grass, if possible. The baby should start to eat grass about now. It may also eat rolled oats, carrots, or chunks of sweet potato or sweet corn. But these should be treats, not its main diet.

4. Play and discovery

Give the baby dirt to dig and play in and branches to gnaw, and make sure it gets lots of walks on grass and through bushland, so it learns about space and scents and terrain. Don't let the baby go out in the sun. It can die of heat prostration or get dry skin, which may get infected.

Play with the baby as much as possible. Rough-and-tumble games like tug of war will develop its muscles and coordination. Let the baby follow you around the garden or anywhere that is safe from dogs and cars.

Don't punish a wombat. You can't train a wombat, but you can scare it. A hurt wombat will learn to fear you. It won't learn not to poop on the stairs, or eat the cat's food, or dig through the dining room floor, or crash through your bedroom door if it's lonely.

The joy—and despair—of living with a wombat is accommodating your life to a wombat's needs and desires.

BACK INTO THE WILD

When an orphan wombat is about a year old, it needs to return to the wild. But a baby wombat that's been brought up by people will die if it's just set loose in the bush. It has to learn how to find wombat burrows, food, and water. So it needs a place like ours, near the bush, where it can live for a few months or a year, where there are caring people who will look after it. It needs a halfway house, where it can learn that wombats don't always sleep on sofas and that the best wombat food doesn't come from cupboards.

Some wombats stay with us for a few weeks and then wander off into the bush; others stay for years. Mostly they stay until they're about eighteen months old, slowly padding off for longer and longer trips away from home, until one day we realize it's been months since we last saw them, and we may never see them again.

(13)

Protecting Wombats

Wombats are not endangered, but in many areas of Australia they're disappearing. If there are too few wombats in a particular location, there won't be enough adults to breed another healthy generation.

WHAT THREATENS WOMBATS?

1. Cars

Wombats like eating along the sides of the road. Cattle and sheep usually don't graze there, so there's little competition for the grass. Also, the moisture from dew or rain that falls on the road washes onto the sides, so even in dry periods there's often a bit of green grass. Wombats will never learn to be careful of cars because they can't smell a car approaching. By the time they do smell it, the car is on them.

2. Too many cattle, horses, or sheep in a paddock

Cattle, sheep, and horses eat the wombat's food, and their heavy feet can flatten wombat burrows.

3. Land fenced off for gardens, farms, or livestock

At our farm we work out ways to grow fruit and vegetables *and* welcome wombats, wallabies, and other wild animals. But most farming methods aren't friendly to such creatures.

No fence stops a wombat. If it can't push through the fence, it will tunnel underneath it. If you've spent days putting in a fence to keep rabbits out or lambs in, it will take a wombat only a few minutes to undo all your good work. The answer to this is a wombat gate.

You can make a swinging gate out of wood and wire and place it across the hole the wombat made in the fence. Or try an old car tire filled with fencing wire. Tie the tire

to the top of the hole. It'll block rabbits and lambs, but a strong wombat will be able to push it aside easily.

Another solution is to push an old six-foot-long culvert pipe through the hole a wombat has dug underneath a fence. Wombats will go down it happily, but other creatures won't like to crawl that far.

4. Fire

Fire is a terrible threat to wombats. They can suffocate in their burrows. Their burrows may be damaged because burnt ground is more likely to collapse. And they can starve if all their grass has been burned.

5. Illegal activities

In Australia it's against the law to kill native animals, but wombats frequently die from eating poisoned grain and bait meant for invasive imported animals—like rabbits. They are also maimed or killed by wild-dog traps. And many are shot by farmers because they make holes in fences or because the farmers feel that wild animals have no place on their land.

6. Ticks and mange

Wombats are attacked by ticks that suck their blood. Mostly they don't seem bothered by this, except when they're poorly fed or stressed in other ways. At these times, the added burden of having ticks can kill them.

Most wombats get mange at some time. A very small insect—*Sarcoptes scabei*—burrows into the wombat's skin to lay its eggs. The itch this creates is agonizing. A wombat will scratch so hard that it tears its skin, and the scratches can become infected or maggot-ridden. Great mange crusts form all over the wombat's body. Its eyes may be so crusty it can't see, and its ears may be so misshapen it can't hear.

Mange is spread from wombat to wombat, usually in an infected wombat burrow; it is also spread by dogs, dingoes, and foxes.

If you live around wombats, as we do, you'll always see a few with bad mange—and it's heartbreaking to watch them suffer. Luckily, there are ways to help. Mange can be treated with medicine that's added to a wombat's food. But it's difficult to do this unless you are feeding the wombat regularly. Mange can also be treated with medicine in a lotion that is poured on the wombat's back. Wombats really dislike this, and after you've done it once, they will keep well away from you when they smell the lotion again!

I've found that the easiest way to treat a wombat for mange is with medicine loaded into a pump-action water pistol. You figure out the correct dose for your wombat, based on its approximate weight. Then you spray the

wombat with the water pistol! Aim at the wombat's back or its side—not its head and certainly not anywhere near its eyes. You will need to repeat this, and perhaps treat the burrow, too.

(14)

Learning from Wombats

My husband and I live in a stone house we built ourselves, with a homemade waterwheel and solar panels to power our home (and computers). Our garden rambles over about 10 acres, with 800 fruit trees and about 270 different kinds of fruit—not counting the 130 varieties of apple. So there's never a time when there isn't fruit to pick.

Human beings evolved with lots of animals around them, and with trees and flowers and other living things. I know that when I'm in a city, surrounded only by people and their products, I find life very limited. I find it much richer when there are wild animals living their own lives around me. I share my land with wild animals, mostly for myself, because without other species I would be less.

It is a privilege to live alongside wild animals. Being able to walk among the fruit trees and watch the wombats and wallabies and kangaroos graze is one of the great joys of my life.

I've spent more than thirty years studying the wombats in my valley, and I've learned a great deal about them—and from them. When a wombat sees the land, it can smell yesterday as well as today . . . and maybe last year, too. Try to see the world the way a wombat does. Know your land well enough to look at the past; then try to see the future. When I make a decision now, I think: What would a wombat do? I believe we'd all benefit if we asked this question: Will this make the world a better place for wombats?

WHAT I'VE LEARNED FROM WOMBATS

- Never lose an opportunity to have a scratch or eat a carrot.

- Odors can be interesting—and so can droppings!

- Be determined. Very determined.

- Enjoy every second of now.

- Know your land and love it.

- Think things through slowly before you make a move; then charge!